Write Chinese With Betty

Betty Hung

Greenwood Press

GREENWOOD PRESS

47 Pokfulam Road, Basement, Hong Kong.

Telephone: 2546 8212

First published June, 1997.

ISBN 962-279-180-8

PRINTED IN HONG KONG BY
NGAI SHING PRINTING CO.

Preface

This is a book for beginners to learn how to write Chinese characters. Step-by-step, the book takes students through the basic strokes used in writing Chinese characters, the order in which the strokes are drawn and then the way in which the strokes make up the structure of Chinese characters. With practice, students will learn how characters are formed, and how to write them properly. By using this book, students will also learn enough to know how to read and write many more Chinese characters not included here. For the book offers a number of ways of looking up a Chinese character in a dictionary: for example, by its "radical" (more of which later), by the number of strokes employed, or by Pinyin or Cantonese romanisation.

Some 144 characters are covered in this book, in 12 lessons. Each lesson is divided into three sections. The first introduces 12 characters, each with Pinyin and Cantonese romanisation, radical, stroke order and English meaning. Rules and hints about writing are given as the student moves along. The second section deals with common phrases that use the characters under study. At the end of each lesson, there are exercises to help the phrases stick. There is a key to these lessons at the back of the book.

The phrases of this book are all from standard Mandarin. True, Cantonese romanisation is provided, too. But that is simply meant as a supplement to help those (few) students primarily learning Cantonese rather than Mandarin. There are many expressions in colloquial Cantonese that are not found in Mandarin. But such expressions have been left out of this book. The keen student of Cantonese can listen out in everyday speech for the Cantonese equivalent of some of the Mandarin expressions that he or she will learn in the following pages.

At the end, there is a set of flash cards showing all the characters in this book, and how they are written. Students can cut these cards out to practise reading and forming characters. At the end, too, characters are also shown in their "simplified" forms, where they apply. In mainland China, there are about 1,000 characters in all that are found in "simplified" forms, in contrast to the "complex" characters used in Taiwan and Hong Kong.

I hope that students will find this book a fun way to learn Chinese characters.

Content

Putonghua Pinyin System

Each syllable of Pinyin is composed of three elements:

1. Initial: the beginning sound element of a syllable. There are 21 initials in all.

2. Final: the ending sound element of a syllable or a vowel. There are 36 finals in all.

3. Tone: the relative pitch, or variation of pitch, of a syllable. There are 4 tones in all.

An example of a syllable:

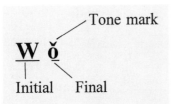

Initials

	as in English			as in English
1. B	bay		12. N	near
2. C	cat's		13. P	pay
3. Ch	chair		14. Q	cheese
4. D	dear		15. R	measure
5. F	fee		16. S	say
6. G	girl		17. Sh	show
7. H	height		18. T	tear
8. J	gee		19. X	she
9. K	keen		20. Z	dad's
10. L	lean		21. Zh	jar
11. M	may			

Finals

	as in English			as in English
1. a	f<u>a</u>ther		19. iong	no equivalent
2. ai	<u>ai</u>sle		20. iu	<u>ill</u>
3. an	<u>au</u>nt		21. o	m<u>o</u>re
4. ang	s<u>ound</u>		22. ong	z<u>one</u>
5. ao	<u>owl</u>		23. ou	t<u>oe</u>
6. e	h<u>er</u>		24. u	r<u>u</u>le
7. ei	d<u>ay</u>		25. ua	g<u>ua</u>va
8. en	no equivalent		26. uai	<u>wide</u>
9. eng	no equivalent		27. uan	<u>wa</u>nt (American accent)
10. er	<u>err</u> (American accent)		28. uang	no equivalent
11. i	mach<u>i</u>ne		29. uen	no equivalent
12. ia	<u>y</u>ah		30. ueng	no equivalent
13. ian	<u>y</u>en		31. ui	no equivalent
14. iang	no equivalent		32. uo	<u>wall</u>
15. iao	no equivalent		33. ü	ü (German)
16. ie	<u>y</u>es		34. üan	no equivalent
17. in	<u>seen</u>		35. üe	no equivalent
18. ing	no equivalent		36. ün	no equivalent

Tones

	Tone Mark	Example
1st tone	with "‐" on top of last vowel	xī
2nd tone	with "ˊ" on top of last vowel	xí
3rd tone	with "ˇ" on top of first vowel	xǐ
4th tone	with "ˋ" on top of last vowel	xì

Cantonese Romanization System

Each syllable of Cantonese is composed of three elements:

1. Initial: the beginning sound element of a syllable. There are 19 initials in all.

2. Final: the ending sound element of a syllable or a vowel. There are 51 finals in all.

3. Tone: the relative pitch, or variation of pitch, of a syllable. There are 7 tones in all.

An example of a syllable:

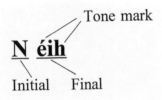

Initials

	as in English		as in English
1. B	boy	11. L	law
2. Ch	chat	12. M	mother
3. D	dog	13. N	nose
4. F	far	14. Ng	singer
5. G	game	15. P	park
6. Gw	language	16. S	sand
7. H	home	17. T	tap
8. J	gypsy	18. W	water
9. K	kill	19. Y	yes
10. Kw	quite		

Finals

	as in English			as in English
1. a	father		27. eut	no equivalent
2. aai	aisle		28. i	bee
3. aak	ark		29. ik	sick
4. aam	arm		30. im	seem
5. aan	aunt		31. in	seen
6. aang	no equivalent		32. ing	king
7. aap	harp		33. ip	jeep
8. aat	art		34. it	seat
9. aau	owl		35. iu	seal
10. ai	kite		36. o	oral
11. ak	duck		37. oi	boy
12. am	sum		38. ok	sock
13. an	sun		39. on	on
14. ang	dung		40. ong	song
15. ap	up		41. ot	odd
16. at	but		42. ou	toe
17. au	out		43. u	fool
18. e	yes		44. ui	"oo" + "ee"
19. ei	day		45. uk	hook
20. ek	echo		46. un	soon
21. eng	bang		47. ung	zone
22. eu	her		48. ut	foot
23. eui	no equivalent		49. yu	no equivalent
24. euk	turk		50. yun	no equivalent
25. eun	no equivalent		51. yut	no equivalent
26. eung	no equivalent			

Tones

	Tone Mark	Example
High level	with "-" on top of first vowel	sī
High Falling	with "`" on top of first vowel	sì
High Rising	with "´" on top of first vowel	sí
Middle Level	none	si
Low Level	With an "h" after the vowel	sih
Low Rising	with "´" on top of first vowel, and an "h" after the vowel	síh
Low Falling	with "`" on top of the first vowel, and an "h" after the vowel	sìh

Lesson 1 **Basic strokes** (1)

一二三十工上正千午牛生年

A horizontal stroke is called "横 héng/wàahng". Write it from left to right, with the right end slightly higher than the left. It is heavy at both ends.

Words to learn

		Radical	*Meaning*	*Notes*
1. 一	yī yāt	一	one	

一

2. 二	èr yih	二	two	Write from top to bottom. The bottom stroke is longer than the top one.

一二

	Radical	Meaning	Notes

3.　三　sān
　　　　sàam　　　　一　　　three　　The middle stroke is slightly shorter than the the top one. The space between the strokes should be even.

一 二 三

A vertical stroke is called " 直 zhí/jihk ". Write from top to bottom. It could be heavy or light at the end. Always write horizontal strokes before vertical ones, except when the horizontal strokes are in the lower part of the character.

Words to learn

	Radical	Meaning	Notes

4.　十　shí
　　　　sahp　　　　十　　　ten　　The end of the vertical stroke is light.

一 十

5.   工   gōng   工   work, job
         gūng

一 丁 工

工						

6.   上   shàng   一   upper, go up   The short horizontal stroke starts from the
         shǎng   middle of the vertical stroke.
         seuhng
         séuhng

丨 卜 上

上						

7.   正   zhèng   正   just, correct
         jīng

一 丁 下 正 正

正						

3

A left-falling stroke is called "撇 piě/pit". It starts from the top and strikes to the left. Lift lightly at the end. It should be smoothly curved. If it is at the top of a character, it is always the first stroke.

Words to learn

		Radical	Meaning		Notes

8. 千 qiān chìn 十 thousand

ノ 二 千

千							

9. 午 wǔ nǵh 十 noon

ノ ⺊ 上 午

午							

		Radical	Meaning	Notes

10.　牛　niú　牛　　cow
　　　　　ngàuh

ノ　ㅗ　二　牛

牛							

11.　生　shēng　生　give birth to,　The second horizontal stroke is slightly shorter.
　　　　sàng;　　　grow
　　　　sàang

ノ　ㅗ　ᄂ　牛　生

生							

12.　年　nián　干　year
　　　　nìhn

ノ　ㅗ　ᄂ　ᄂ　ᄐ　年

年							

Phrases to learn

		Romanization	Meaning
1.	十一	shí yī sahp yāt	eleven
2.	十二	shí èr sahp yih	twelve
3.	二十	èr shí yih sahp	twenty
4.	二十三	èr shí sān yih sahp sàam	twenty three
5.	三十	sān shí sàam sahp	thirty
6.	一千	yī qiān yāt chìn	one thousand
7.	上午	shàng wǔ seuhng nǵh	forenoon; morning
8.	正午	zhèng wǔ jing nǵh	high noon
9.	一生	yī shēng yāt sàng	all one's life
10.	十年	shí nián sahp nìhn	ten years

Exercise

I. Choose the correct stroke order

1. a) 一 二 工   b) 丿 丁 工
   c) 一 丁 工   d) 一 丄 工

2. a) 一 丅 下 圧 正　　b) 丨 丁 下 圧 正
   c) 一 丁 工 王 正　　d) 一 丁 圷 圧 正

3. a) 丨 十 𦍌 主 生　　b) 丿 丩 牛 牛 生
   c) 丿 𠂉 𠂆 牛 生　　d) 丿 𠂉 牛 牛 生

4. a) 一 𠂉 二 二 三 年　　b) 丿 𠂉 二 二 三 年
   c) 丿 𠂉 二 二 午 年　　d) 一 𠂉 个 午 午 年

II. Choose the best meaning of the phrases

5. 二千年
   a) two hundred years　　b) two thousand years
   c) twenty years　　d) two years

6. 上午
   a) 3:00 - 6:00 am.　　b) 9:00 - 12:00 am.
   c) 12:00 - 2:00 am.　　d) 5:00 - 8:00 pm.

7. 三十一
   a) thirteen　　b) thirty
   c) thirty two　　d) thirty one

8. 十年
   a) ten years　　b) ten lives
   c) twelve years　　d) ten thousand

III. Matching

9. 工   •   •   a) three years

10. 上 午   •   •   b) morning

11. 一 生   •   •   c) one thousand years

12. 二 千   •   •   d) job

13. 正 午   •   •   e) all one's life

14. 一 千 年   •   •   f) two thousand

15. 三 年   •   •   g) noon

IV. Dictation

16. cow _____

17. twenty two _____

18. three thousand years _____

19. grow _____

20. just _____

8

Lesson 2 **Basic strokes** (2)

八人入大天下太主文六半火

A right-falling stroke is called "捺 nà/naaht ". It starts from top left, and falls to the right. Push down at the bottom then lift up. The left-falling stroke should be written before the right-falling stroke.

Words to learn

	Radical	Meaning	Notes
1. 八 bā baat	八	eight	The two strokes should not touch.

丿 八

八							

	Radical	Meaning	Notes
2. 人 rén yàhn	人	people	The right-falling stroke starts from middle of the left-falling stroke.

丿 人

人							

	Radical	Meaning	Notes

3. 入   rù   入   enter, join   The left-falling stroke touches the right-falling stroke at the middle.
     yahp

丿 入

入							

4. 大   dà   大   big
     daaih

一 ナ 大

大							

5. 天   tiān   大   sky
     tīn

一 二 于 天

天							

A dot is called "點 diǎn/dím". It could fall to the left or right. If it is on the left, it should be heavy at the end. If it is on the top right, it is like a short left-falling stroke. If it is on bottom right, it is heavy at the end. A dot is either the first or the last stroke.

Words to learn

		Radical	*Meaning*	*Notes*
6.	下 xià hah	一	below, go down	The dot is the last stroke.

一 丅 下

下								

7.	太 tài taai	大	too much, wife, Mrs.	The dot is the last stroke.

一 ナ 大 太

太								

| | Radical | Meaning | Notes |

8. 主 zhǔ / jyú ` host, owner, main

` 一 二 宇 主

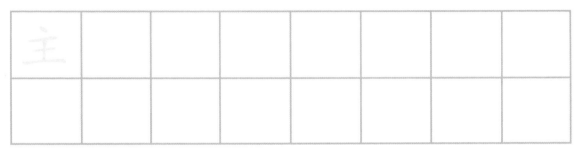

9. 文 wén / màhn 文 language, writing, a surname — The left-falling and right-falling stroke cross at the centre of the character.

` 一 ナ 文

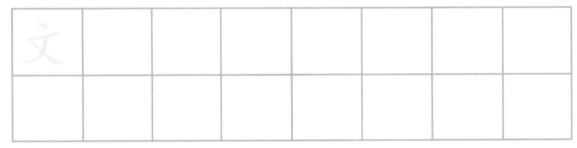

10. 六 liù / luhk 八 six

` 一 六 六

		Radical	Meaning		Notes

11. 半 bàn / bun 十 half Write the two dots on top first. The right dot is like a short left-falling stroke.

丶 丷 半 半 半

半							

12. 火 huǒ / fó 火 fire

丶 ⺍ 少 火

火							

Phrases to learn

		Romanization	Meaning
1.	八十六	bā shí liù baat sahp luhk	eighty six
2.	人人	rén rén yàhn yàhn	everbody, everyone
3.	大人	dà rén daaih yàhn	adult
4.	工人	gōng rén gūng yàhn	worker

5.	主人	zhǔ rén jyú yàhn	master, host, owner
6.	人生	rén shēng yàhn sàng	life
7.	一天	yī tiān yāt tīn	one day
8.	天天	tiān tiān tīn tīn	everyday
9.	下午	xià wǔ hah ńgh	afternoon
10.	太大	tài dà taai daaih	too big
11.	太太	tài tai taai táai	wife, Mrs., madamn
12.	大半	dà bàn daaih bun	more than half, greater part
13.	半年	bàn nián bun nìhn	half year

Exercise

I. Choose the correct stroke order

1.   a) 一 二 于 天   b) 丿 人 一 天
      c) 一 丁 于 天   d) 一 二 于 天

2.   a) 丶 二 文 文   b) 丶 二 才 文
      c) 一 二 才 文   d) 一 丁 又 文

3.   a) 丶 丶 丷 半 半   b) 丨 丨 丷 半 半
      c) 丷 丷 半 半 半   d) 丶 丷 半 半 半

4. a) ` ⼧ ⼗ ⼲ 主   b) ` ⼆ ⼆ ⼲ 主
    c) ` ⼆ ⼗ ⼲ 主   d) ⼀ ⼆ ⼲ 王 主

II. Choose the best meaning of the phrases

5. 六十天
    a) sixty   b) sixty days
    c) six years   d) sixty workers

6. 半年
    a) half year   b) one and a half year
    c) coming six months   d) last six months

7. 大火
    a) gentle heat   b) big half
    c) strong heat   d) small half

8. 工人
    a) scholars   b) adult
    c) wife   d) workers

9. 上下
    a) forenoon   b) on top
    c) above and below   d) at the bottom

10. 八千年
    a) eight thousand years   c) ten thousand years
    c) eighty years   d) ten more years

III. Matching

11. 下午 •   • a) six thousand people

12. 天天 •   • b) three and a half years

13. 大人 •   • c) everybody

14. 六千人 •   • d) adult

15. 人人 •   • e) more than half

16. 三年半 •   • f) afternoon

17. 大半 •   • g) everday

18. 文太太 •   • h) Mrs. Wen/Man

VI. Dictation

19. fire   _____

20. life   _____

21. too big   _____

22. ten and a half days   _____

23. enter   _____

24. owner   _____

Lesson 3 **Basic strokes** (3)

口中日百五七出友名女公去

An elbow is called " 彎 wān/wāan ". It is formed by two strokes with a pause in between.

Words to learn

		Radical	Meaning	Notes

A. ㄱ

1. 口　kǒu háu　　口　mouth　The elbow is formed by a horizontal stroke and a vertical stroke.

丶 冂 口

口							

2. 中　zhōng jùng　丨　middle, centre　The vertical stroke is the last stroke.

丶 冂 口 中

中							

17

| | | *Radical* | *Meaning* | *Notes* |

3. 日　rì　日　day, sun
　　　　yaht

丨 冂 冂 日

日							

4. 百　bǎi　白　hundred
　　　　baak

一 丆 丆 丆 百 百

百							

5. 五　wǔ　二　five　The vertical stroke and the elbow fall slightly to the
　　　　ńgh　　　　　　left.

一 丁 开 五

五							

		Radical	Meaning		Notes

B. ㄥ

6. 七   qī   chāt   一   seven   The elbow should turn smoothly. In hand writing, there is no hook at the end of the elbow.

一 七

七							

7. 出   chū   chēut   凵   out   Write the vertical stroke first. The elbow is formed by a vertical stroke and a horizontal stroke.

ㄥ 凵 屮 出 出

出							

C. フ

8. 友   yǒu   yáuh   又   friend   The elbow is formed by a horizontal stroke and a left-falling stroke.

一 ナ 方 友

友							

19

	Radical	*Meaning*	*Notes*

9.　名　míng　口　name, famous
　　　　mìhng

ノ ク タ 夕 名 名

名							

D. ㄑ

10.　女　nǔ　女　female,
　　　　néuih　　woman,
　　　　　　　　daughter

The first and second stroke cross at the centre line of the character.

ㄑ 夂 女

女						

E. ㄥ

11.　公　gōng　八　public,
　　　　gūng　　grandfather

The elbow is formed by a left-falling stroke and a horizontal stroke, end up lightly.

ノ 八 公 公

公						

	Radical	Meaning	Notes

12. 去 qù heui 　土　　go

一 十 土 去 去

Phrases to learn

		Romanization	Meaning
1.	人口	rén kǒu yàhn háu	population
2.	入口	rù kǒu yahp háu	entrance
3.	出口	chū kǒu chēut háu	exit, export
4.	出去	chū qù chēut heui	go out
5.	出生	chū shēng chēut sāng	be born
6.	生日	shēng rì sàng yaht	birthday
7.	中文	zhōng wén jùng màhn	Chinese language
8.	中午	zhōng wǔ jūng ńgh	noon; midday

9.	中年	zhōng nián jùng nìhn	middle age
10.	五百七十	wǔ bǎi qī shí ńgh baak chāt sahp	five hundred and seventy
11.	友人	yǒu rén yáuh yàhn	friend
12.	女人	nǚ rén néuih yán	woman
13.	公主	gōng zhǔ gūng jyú	princess
14.	去年	qù nián heui nìhn	last year

Exercise

I. Choose the correct stroke order

1.   a) 一 丁 丙 五   b) 丿 丁 工 五
       c) 丿 力 丙 五   d) 丿 丁 丙 五

2.   a) 𠃋 厶 公 公   b) 丿 八 公 公
       c) 乀 八 公 公   d) 丿 厶 公 公

3.   a) 丨 十 土 去 去   b) 一 十 土 去 去
       c) 一 十 土 去 去   d) 一 二 土 去 去

4.   a) 丿 ク 夕 夕 名 名   b) 丿 ク 夕 名 名 名
       c) 丿 く 夕 夕 名 名   d) 丿 ク 夕 名 名 名

II. Choose the best meaning of the phrases

5. 七百年
   a) seven thousand years
   b) seventeen years
   c) seven hundred years
   d) Year 700

6. 入口
   a) population
   b) entrance
   c) exit
   d) import

7. 七千三百五十二
   a) 7532
   b) 5732
   c) 7253
   d) 7352

8. 中午
   a) 上午
   b) 正午
   c) 下午
   d) 中文

9. Woman
   a) 女大
   b) 女入
   c) 女八
   d) 女人

10. Middle age
    a) 大年
    b) 下年
    c) 年日
    d) 中年

III. Matching

11. 一百八十 • • a) princess

12. 生日 • • b) last year

13. 公主 • • c) hostess

14. 下去 • • d) birthday

15. 人口 • • e) Chinese language

16. 去年 • • f) go down

17. 中文 • • g) population

18. 女主人 • • h) one hundred and eighty

IV. Dictation

19. friend _____

20. 2857 days _____

21. entrance _____

22. Chinese language _____

23. be born _____

24. go out _____

Lesson 4 Basic strokes (4)

小可衣你心元先月司方九以

A hook is called " 勾 gōu/ngāu ". It may appear at the bottom of a vertical stroke, at the end of a horizontal stroke or an elbow.

Words to learn

	Radical	Meaning	Notes

A. 亅

1. 小   xiǎo   小   little, small
       síu

亅 小 小

小							

2. 可   kě   口   can, approve,
      hó   be worth

一 丆 一 可 可

可							

B. ㇈

3. 衣 yī / yī   衣   clothing

丶 亠 ナ ナ 衣 衣

衣							

C. 亠

4. 你 nǐ / néih   人   you   Write the from left section to right section. The hook is at the end of a horizontal stroke.

ノ 亻 亻 伫 伫 你 你

你							

D. ㇃

5. 心 xīn / sām   心   heart, mind   Write from left to right.

丶 心 心 心

心						

E. 凵

6. 元　yuán　儿　dollar　The elbow should turn smoothly. In hand
　　　yùhn　　　　　　writing, the second horizontal is usually link
　　　　　　　　　　　with the left-falling stroke like an elbow.

一 二 テ 元

元							

7. 先　xiān　儿　first, before,
　　　sīn　　　　　earlier

丿 ㇒ 屮 生 屮 先

先							

F. 冂

8. 月　yuè　月　month, moon
　　　yuht

丿 刀 月 月

月							

		Radical	Meaning		Notes

9. 司   sī   口   take charge
         sī   of

⼕ ⼕ 刁 司 司

10. 方   fāng   方   square,   The elbow should turn smoothly.
         fōng   direction

丶 亠 方 方

G. 乙

11. 九   jiǔ   乙   nine
         gáu

丿 九

 A tick is called "挑 tiǎo/tìu". It is usually at the bottom left.

	Radical	Meaning	Notes
12. 以 yǐ / yíh	人	use, take	

ｌ　ｙ　ｙ゙　以　以

以							

Phrases to learn

		Romanization	Meaning
1.	大小	dà xiǎo daaih síu	size
2.	小心	xiǎo xīn síu sām	be careful, take care
3.	中心	zhōng xīn jūng sām	centre
4.	可口	kě kǒu hó háu	tasty, good to eat
5.	可以	kě yǐ hó yíh	can, allow

6.	以上	yǐ shàng yíh seuhng	above
7.	以下	yǐ xià yíh hah	below; under
8.	上衣	shàng yī seuhng yī	jacket
9.	大衣	dà yī daaih yī	overcoat
10.	九元	jiǔ yuán gáu yùhn	nine dollars
11.	先生	xiān sheng sīn sāang	teacher, Mr., gentleman
12.	一月一日	yī yuè yī rè yāt yuht yāt yaht	1st of January
13.	上月	shàng yuè seuhng yuht	last month
14.	下月	xià yuè hah yuht	next month
15.	公司	gōng sī gūng sī	company, corporation
16.	上司	shàng si seuhng sī	boss; superior

Exercise

I. Choose the correct stroke order

1. a) ノ 一 十 牛 牛 先
    b) ノ 一 二 牛 牛 先
    c) 一 十 牛 牛 牛 先
    d) ノ 一 十 牛 牜 先

2. a) 一 丁 丁 可 可   b) 丨 丁 丁 可 可

    c) 丶 宀 口 日 可   d) 一 宀 冖 日 可

3. a) 乚 心 心 心   b) 乚 心 心 心

    c) 丶 八 心 心   d) 丶 心 心 心

4. a) ノ 夕 夕 尔 你   b) 丨 亻 仁 你 你 你

    c) ノ 亻 亻 你 你 你   d) ノ 亻 亻 你 你 你

5. a) 丶 亠 亠 才 衣 衣   b) 丶 亠 六 才 衣 衣

    c) 一 ブ 才 不 衣 衣   d) 丶 亠 六 才 衣 衣

II. Choose the best meaning of the phrases

6. $900

    a) 九百元   b) 百九元

    c) 元九百   d) 元百九

7. Mr. Wen/Man

    a) 文先牛   b) 文太太

    c) 文先生   d) 文元主

8. More than 50 days

    a) 五天以上   b) 十五天以下

    c) 五十天以上   d) 五十天以下

9. 你可以出去

    a) You can go out   b) You can go home

    c) You have to go up   d) You have to go down

10. 8th July, 1936

    a) 八日七月一九三六年

    b) 七日八月一九三六年

    c) 七月八日一千九百三十六年

    d) 一九三六年七月八日

11. 上衣太小

    a) The jacket is too long   b) The jacket is too small

    c) The overcoat is too small   d) The overcoat is too big

12. 中心

    a) centre   b) heart

    c) be careful   d) careless

III. Matching

13. 上月   •   •   a) company

14. 十元   •   •   b) last month

15. 九月   •   •   c) September

16. 下月   •   •   d) above

17. 公司   •   •   e) below 20

18. 二十以下   •   •   f) ten dollars

19. 小心   •   •   g) next month

20. 以上   •   •   h) be careful

IV. Dictation

21. 4th of the last month   _____

22. $85   _____

23. tasty   _____

24. overcoat   _____

25. size   _____

V. Write a Chinese character with the given strokes

26. 亠 _____   27. 儿 _____   28. 𠃌 _____

Lesson 5 **Stroke order**

水本來東果車事用肉有雨兩

Firstly write horizontal stroke, secondly write vertical stroke, then write left-falling stroke and right-falling stroke.

Words to learn

		Radical	*Meaning*	*Notes*
1.	水 shuǐ séui	水	water	Start with the vertical stroke in the middle.

丨 氵 水 水

水						

		Radical	*Meaning*	
2.	本 běn bún	木	origin, book	

一 十 才 木 本

本						

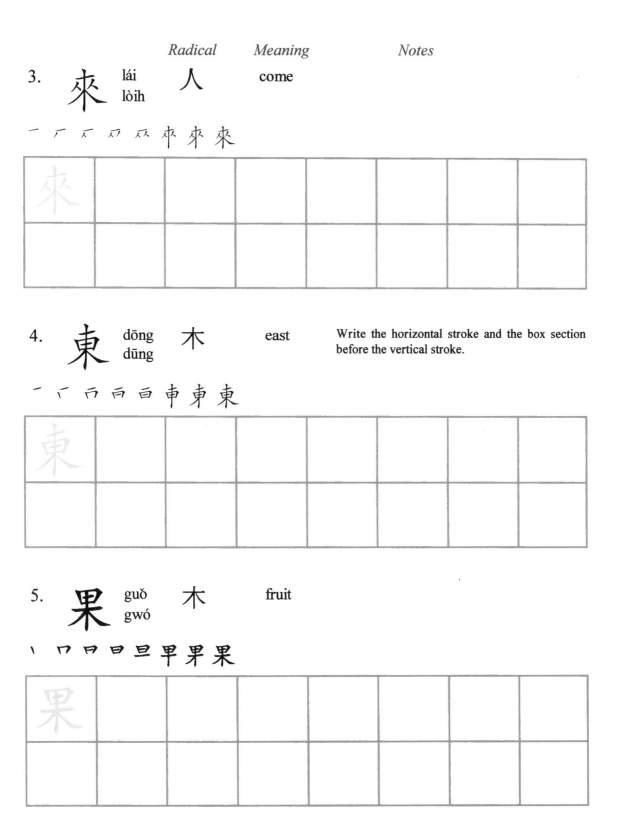

| | | Radical | Meaning | | Notes |

3. 來 lái 人　　come
　　lòih

一 厂 厃 夾 夾 來 來 來

4. 東 dōng 木　　east　　Write the horizontal stroke and the box section
　　dūng　　　　　　before the vertical stroke.

一 厂 厅 百 申 東 東 東

5. 果 guǒ 木　　fruit
　　gwó

丶 口 日 日 旦 甲 果 果

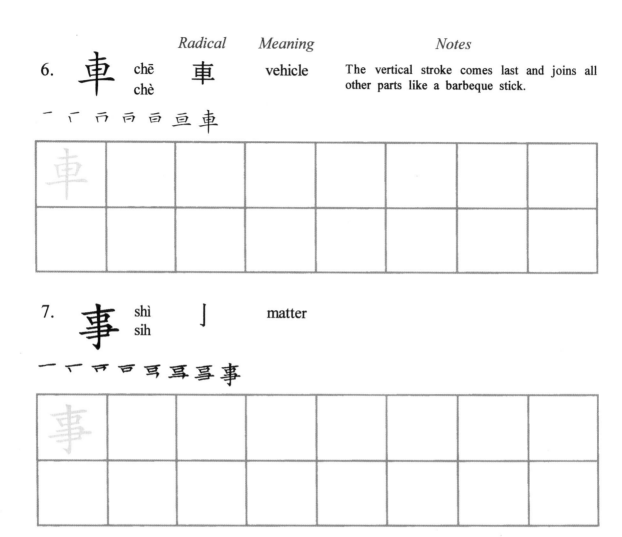

| Radical | Meaning | Notes |

6. 車 chē / chè   車   vehicle   The vertical stroke comes last and joins all other parts like a barbeque stick.

一 厂 厂 亍 百 亘 車

7. 事 shì / sih   亅   matter

一 厂 厂 百 写 写 写 事

Write the outer frame first, then fill the inside in the order top to bottom, left to right.

| | Radical | Meaning | Notes |

8. 用 yòng 用 use
   yuhng

ノ 几 月 月 用

用							

9. 肉 ròu 肉 meat   The frame is a rectangle.
   yuhk

丨 冂 内 内 肉 肉

肉							

10. 有 yǒu 月 have, there is
    yáuh

一 ナ オ 冇 有 有

有							

	Radical	Meaning	Notes

11. 雨 yǔ / yúh   雨   rain   Split the frame into two with the vertical stroke. Fill the left hand section, then the right hand section.

一 丆 丙 币 雨 雨 雨 雨

雨							

12. 兩 liǎng / léuhng   入   two

一 丆 丙 币 雨 雨 兩 兩

兩							

Phrases to learn

		Romanization	Meaning
1.	水果	shuǐ guǒ séui gwó	fruit
2.	日本	rì běn yaht bún	Japan
3.	本事	běn shì bún sih	ability, capable
4.	本來	běn lái bún lòih	originally, original

5.	出來	chū lái chēut lòih	come out
6.	東方	dōng fāng dūng fōng	the east, the Orient
7.	火車	huǒ chē fó chè	train
8.	有用	yǒu yòng yáuh yuhng	useful
9.	用心	yòng xīn yuhng sām	with concentrated attention, diligently
10.	有名	yǒu míng yáuh mìhng	famous, well-known
11.	有一天	yǒu yī tiān yáuh yāt tīn	some day, on one day
12.	牛肉	niú ròu ngàuh yuhk	beef
13.	下雨	xià yǔ hah yúh	(V) rain
14.	兩年	liǎng nián léuhng nìhn	two years

Exercise

I. Choose the correct stroke order

1. a) 丿 冂 月 月 用 b) 丿 𠃊 𠂉 月 用
    c) 𠃌 冂 月 月 用 d) 丿 冂 爪 爪 用

2. a) 丨 十 才 木 本 b) 一 十 才 木 本
    c) 丨 十 𠦝 才 本 d) 一 十 𠦝 才 本

3.   a) フ 刀 水 水   b) ｜ 广 ㇄ 水
           c) フ ㇇ ㇄ 水   d) ｜ 刀 水 水

4.   a) ｜ ｜ 『 甲 甲 里 果   b) 丶 口 曰 日 甲 甲 里 果
           c) 丶 口 曰 日 旦 甲 里 果   d) 丶 口 曰 日 旦 臾 昊 果

5.   a) ｜ 冂 内 内 肉 肉   b) ｜ 冂 冂 内 肉 肉
           c) ノ 人 夕 歺 歺 肉   d) 冂 冂 内 内 肉 肉

II. Count the number of strokes of the following characters

6. 事   7. 東   8. 兩   9. 來   10. 有

III. Choose the best meaning of the phrases

11.   two years

     a) 倆年   b) 三年
     c) 兩年   d) 年二

12.   oriental people

     a) 東方人   b) 果方入
     c) 車方人   d) 東方入

13.   fruit

     a) 水東   b) 小果
     c) 本果   d) 水果

14.   originally

     a) 本來   b) 上來
     c) 正本   d) 出來

15.　useful

a) 有名　　　　　　　b) 有用

c) 有心　　　　　　　d) 用心

IV. Matching

16.　出來　　　·　　　　·　　a) Japan

17.　雨天　　　·　　　　·　　b) capability

18.　水　　　·　　　　·　　c) come out

19.　日本　　　·　　　　·　　d) rainny day

20.　有名　　　·　　　　·　　e) water

21.　本事　　　·　　　　·　　f) famous

V. Dictation

22. beef　　　_____

23. two and a half years　　_____

24. Japanese people　　_____

25. raining　　_____

26. train　　_____

Lesson 6 Box structure & layer structure (1)

回四西面今字家寫空常早星

When writing characters which look like a box, firstly write the outer frame, but leave out the bottom line. Fill the box, and finally close the box with a horizontal stroke.

Words to learn

		Radical	*Meaning*	*Notes*

1. 回   huí   wùih   口   return, back, reply

丨 冂 冂 冋 冋 囬 回

回						

2. 四   sì   sei   口   four

丨 冂 冂 四 四

四						

3. 西 xī   西   west
        sāi

一 丆 币 丙 西 西

4. 面 miàn   面   face, surface   When writing the tube inside the box, firstly
        mihn   write the vertical strokes on both sides, then fill
                                      in the horizontal strokes.

一 丆 丆 丙 而 而 而 面 面

The structure of some characters is divided
into layers. Write from top to bottom, layer
by layer.

| | | Radical | Meaning | | Notes |

5.　今 jīn　人　today, now
　　　 gām

ノ 人 仒 今

今							

6.　字 zì　子　word,
　　　 jih　　character

丶 丷 宀 宁 宁 字

字						

7.　家 jiā　宀　home
　　　 gā

丶 丷 宀 宀 宁 宁 穷 家 家 家

家					

44

	Radical	Meaning	Notes

8. 寫 xiě 宀 write
sé

丶丷宀宀宀宀宀宀宀宀宀宀寫寫寫寫寫

寫							

9. 空 kōng 穴 empty, vacant
kòng
hùng

丶丷宀宀穴空空空

空							

10. 常 cháng 巾 often
sèuhng

丶丷丷丷丷丷常常常常常常

常							

		Radical	Meaning	Notes

11. 早 zǎo / jóu 日 early, morning

丶 冂 日 日 旦 早

早							

12. 星 xīng / sīng 日 star

丶 冂 日 日 旦 旦 早 星

星							

Phrases to learn

		Romanization	Meaning
1.	四方	sì fāng / sei fōng	square, cubic
2.	東西	dōng xi / dūng sāi	thing
3.	西面	xī miàn / sāi mihn	west side
4.	回來	huí lái / wùih lòih	come back

5.	回家	huí jiā wùih gā	go home
6.	家人	jiā rén gā yàhn	family member
7.	大家	dà jiā daaih gā	all of us
8.	今天	jīn tiān gām tīn	today
9.	文字	wén zì màhn jih	characters, writing
10.	名字	míng zì mìhng jih	name
11.	寫字	xiě zì sé jih	to write (words)
12.	天空	tiān kōng tīn hūng	sky
13.	有空	yǒu kòng yáuh hùng	have time, at leisure
14.	常常	cháng cháng sèuhng sèuhng	often
15.	正常	zhèng cháng jing sèuhng	normal
16.	早上	zǎo shàng jóu seuhng	morning
17.	星星	xīng xīng sīng sīng	star

Exercise

I. Choose the correct stroke order

1. a) 丿 儿 儿 四 四　　　　　　　b) 丨 冂 冂 四 四
    c) 丁 冂 冂 四 四　　　　　　　d) 丨 冂 口 四 四

2. a) 丶 亠 今 今　　　　　　　　b) 丶 人 亼 今
    c) 丿 人 今 今　　　　　　　　d) 丿 人 亼 今

3. a) 丶 冂 日 日 早 早　　　　　b) 丶 冂 日 日 旦 早
    c) 丶 冂 口 日 旦 早　　　　　d) 丶 冂 口 日 早 早

4. a) 丶 丷 宀 宁 宁 字　　　　　b) 乛 了 子 字 字 字
    c) 丶 一 宀 宁 宁 字　　　　　d) 丶 丷 亠 亠 空 字

5. a) 丨 冂 口 曰 回 回　　　　　b) 丶 冂 口 囗 囘 回
    c) 丨 冂 冂 冋 回 回　　　　　d) 丨 卜 冂 冋 囘 回

II. Choose the best meaning of the phrases

6. Today

    a) 雨天　　　　　　　　　　b) 天空
    c) 兩天　　　　　　　　　　d) 今天

7. It rainned this morning

    a) 下雨今天早上　　　　　b) 今天早上下雨
    c) 早上今天雨下　　　　　d) 今天下雨早上

8.   Chinese name

   a) 中文名字   b) 中文文字
   c) 文字中文   d) 名字中文

III. Count the number of strokes of the following characters

9. 寫   10. 星   11. 面   12. 常

IV. Matching

13. 下 面   •   •   a) name

14. 回家   •   •   b) westerner

15. 今早   •   •   c) this morning

16. 寫字   •   •   d) writing

17. 名字   •   •   e) normal

18. 正常   •   •   f) go home

19. 西方人   •   •   g) below

20. 四百   •   •   h) four hundred

V. Fill in the blanks

21.　日本 ＿＿＿＿＿＿ 下雨 。

Japan <u>often</u> rains.

22.　＿＿＿＿＿＿ 上有 ＿＿＿＿＿＿ 。

There are <u>stars</u> in the <u>sky</u> above.

23.　大家 ＿＿＿＿＿＿ 去 。

Let's <u>go home</u>.

VI. Dictation

24. You have time ＿＿＿＿＿＿＿＿＿＿＿＿

25. come back ＿＿＿＿＿＿＿＿＿＿＿＿

26. east side ＿＿＿＿＿＿＿＿＿＿＿＿

27. character ＿＿＿＿＿＿＿＿＿＿＿＿

28. square ＿＿＿＿＿＿＿＿＿＿＿＿

29. write the name ＿＿＿＿＿＿＿＿＿＿＿＿

30. family member ＿＿＿＿＿＿＿＿＿＿＿＿

Lesson 7 Layer structure (2)

分老走市商菜第業男思意美

Words to learn

		Radical	Meaning	Notes

1. 分   fēn   刀   minute, divide, component
   - fen
   - fān
   - fahn

ノ 八 分 分

分							

2. 老   lǎo   老   old, elder
   - lóuh

一 十 土 耂 耂 老

老							

3. 走   zǒu   走   go, walk   The right-falling stroke at the bottom should lie flat as a base.
   - jáu

一 十 土 キ キ 走 走

走						

		Radical	*Meaning*		*Notes*

4. 市   shì   巾   market
      síh

丶 亠 广 方 市

市						

5. 商   shāng   口   business;
      sēung   consult

丶 亠 广 广 产 产 商 商 商

商						

6. 菜   cài   艹   vegetables;
      choi   dish of food

丶 十 艹 艹 芇 芇 芋 芇 芇 荳 苹 莃 菜

菜						

	Radical	Meaning	Notes

7. 第   dì
  daih   竹   ordinal particle

丿 ⺁ ⺮ ⺮ ⺮ 竺 竺 笃 笃 第 第

第						

8. 業   yè
  yihp   木   line of
  business   The top section is a right-falling dot, two short vertical strokes and a left-falling dot.

丨 丨 丨丨 业 业 业 业 业 业 丵 業 業 業

業						

9. 男   nán
  nàahm   田   man, male

丶 冂 冃 冊 田 男 男

男						

	Radical	Meaning	Notes

10. 思 sī / sī 心 think

丶 冂 冃 冊 田 囟 思 思 思

思						

11. 意 yì / yi 心 meaning, intention

丶 亠 亠 立 产 产 音 音 音 意 意 意

意						

12. 美 měi / méih 羊 beautiful

54

丶 ⺌ ⺌ ⺌ ⺌ 羊 羊 美 美

美							

Phrases to learn

		Romanization	*Meaning*
1.	十分	shí fēn sahp fān	(A) very; utterly, extremely (N) ten minutes, ten points or marks
2.	分公司	fēn gōng sī fān gūng sī	branch office of a company
3.	老人	lǎo rén lóuh yàhn	old man or woman
4.	菜市	cài shì choi síh	food market
5.	商人	shāng rén sēung yàhn	merchant
6.	商業	shāng yè sēung yihp	business, commerce
7.	工業	gōng yè gūng yihp	industry
8.	第一	dì yī daih yāt	the first, number one
9.	第一名	dì yī míng daih yāt mìhng	get a first, win a championship

10.	男人	nán rén nàahm yán	man
11.	意思	yì si yi sì	meaning, idea
12.	有意思	yǒu yì si yáuh yi sī	interesting, a lot of fun
13.	主意	zhǔ yì jyú yi	decision, idea
14.	生意	shēng yi sàng yi	business, trade
15.	美人	měi rén méih yàhn	beautiful woman, beauty

Exercise

I. Choose the correct stroke order

1. a) 一 亠 宀 宀 市
   b) 丶 亠 宀 宀 市
   c) 丶 亠 十 市 市
   d) 丶 亠 宀 市 市

2. a) 丿 八 分 分
   b) 丿 八 分 分
   c) 丶 八 分 分
   d) 丁 刀 勹 分

3. a) 一 二 土 耂 老 老
   b) 一 二 土 耂 耂 老
   c) 一 十 土 耂 耂 老
   d) 一 十 土 耂 耂 老

II. Count the number of strokes of the following characters

4. 業   5. 第   6. 美   7. 意

III. Choose the best meaning of the phrases

8.   very careful

a) 十分分心   b) 分心十分

c) 十分小心   d) 小心十分

9.   Japanese merchant

a) 日本商人   b) 百木商人

c) 日文商人   d) 日本商業

10.   the third day

a) 三日   b) 第三天

c) 第三名   d) 三天

11.   export business

a) 出口工業   b) 出口商業

c) 出口生意   d) 出口商人

12.   你上菜市去

a) You go to the market   b) You go up to the market

c) You go to buy vegetables   d) You go up to buy vegetables

IV. Dictation

13. industrial centre   _____

14. go, walk   _____

15. business, trade   _____

16. (score) one hundred mark _____

17. old people _____

18. man _____

V. Matching

19.	男女 •	• a)	interesting
20.	有意思 •	• b)	business
21.	生意 •	• c)	beautiful woman
22.	美女 •	• d)	men and women
23.	主意 •	• e)	idea
24.	分公司 •	• f)	branch office

VI. Fill in the blanks

25. 寫中文很_____。

Write Chinese is very <u>interesting</u>.

26. 水果_____可口。

The fruit is <u>very</u> delicious.

27. 今年是_____。

This year is <u>the fourth year</u>.

Lesson 8 Layer structure (3)

要票坐重書見看買賣專電愛

Words to learn

		Radical	Meaning	Notes

1. 要 yào / yiu   西   want, need, must

一 厂 厂 厉 两 西 要 要 要

2. 票 piào / piu   示   ticket

一 厂 厂 厉 两 西 西 亜 票 票 票

3. 坐 zuò / joh   土   sit

ノ 人 バ 从 丛 坐 坐

坐							

	Radical	Meaning	Notes

4. 重
zhòng
chúhng
juhng
里
heavy,
important

一 二 千 亡 盲 盲 重 重 重

重							

5. 書
shū
syù
曰
book

一 二 ヨ 申 聿 圭 書 書 書 書

書							

6. 見
jiàn
gin
見
see, meet

In hand writing, the bottom horizontal stroke is usually linked with the left-falling stroke, forming an elbow.

｜ 冂 冃 月 目 貝 見

見							

		Radical	Meaning		Notes

7. 看   kàn   目   look, see,
      hon   read

一 二 三 手 手 看 看 看 看

看							

8. 買   mǎi   貝   buy   In hand writing, the bottom horizontal stroke is
      máaih   usually linked with the left dot, forming a short
                           elbow.

丶 冂 冂 罒 罒 罒 罒 買 冒 冒 買 買

買							

9. 賣   mài   貝   sell   In the top section, the first horizontal stroke
      maaih   should be longer than the second one.

一 十 士 士 吉 吉 吉 声 声 声 責 賣 賣 賣

賣						

| | | Radical | Meaning | | | Notes |

10. 專　zhuān　寸　special, expert
　　　jyūn

一 厂 厂 百 百 亩 重 重 重 專 專

專						

11. 電　diàn　雨　electricity, lightning
　　　dihn

In writing the top section, the box is formed by a dot on the left, then a horizontal stroke with a hook at the end.

一 厂 厂 币 币 雨 雨 雪 雪 雪 雷 雷 電

電						

12. 愛　ài　心　love
　　　oi / ngoi

一　ノ　ハ　ヴ　ヴ　严　严　炁　炁　炁　愛　愛　愛

愛						

Phrases to learn

		Romanization	*Meaning*
1.	重要	zhòng yào juhng yiu	important
2.	主要	zhǔ yào jyú yiu	main, chief, major
3.	車票	chē piào chè piu	train or bus ticket
4.	坐下	zuò xià joh hah	sit down
5.	坐車	zuò chē joh chè	travel by car
6.	一本書	yī běn shū yāt bún syù	a book
7.	中文書	zhōng wén shū jùng màhn syù	Chinese book
8.	意見	yì jiàn yi gin	opinion, suggestion, idea, advice
9.	見面	jiàn miàn gin mihn	meet
10.	看見	kàn jiàn hon gin	see, catch sight of

11.	專心	zhuān xīn jyūn sām	concentrate one's attention
12.	專家	zhuān jiā jyūn gā	expert, specialist
13.	專業	zhuān yè jyūn yihp	professional, specialized subject
14.	電車	diàn chē dihn chè	tram, tramcar

Exercise

I. Count the number of strokes

1. 愛　　2. 書　　3. 電　　4. 專

II. Choose the correct stroke order

5. a) ノ 人 朼 朴 坐 丛 丛 坐　　b) ノ 人 朼 朴 坐 丛 坐 坐

c) 丨 亻 시 시 시 坐 坐　　c) 丨 十 土 坐 坐 坐 坐

6. a) 一 二 干 干 甫 甫 甫 甫 重　b) 一 二 千 千 甫 甫 重 重 重

c) 一 二 干 甫 甫 甫 重 重 重　d) 一 丁 千 千 甫 甫 重 重 重

III. Choose the best meaning of the phrases

7. 買車票

a) sell ticket

c) collect ticket

b) buy ticket

d) bus ticket

64

8.   專業意見

   a) business advice   b) special idea

   c) professional advice   d) suggestion for a special purpose

9.   two books

   a) 本二書   b) 三本書
   c) 本兩書   d) 兩本書

10.   go to market to buy things

   a) 買東西去菜市   b) 去菜市買東西
   c) 賣東方去菜市   d) 去菜市賣東西

11.   come back by tram

   a) 坐電車回來   b) 看電車回來
   c) 坐火車去   d) 坐火車去

III. Choose the correct characters for the following English phrases

| 重 | 面 | 心 | 見 | 下 | 要 | 要 | 意 | 坐 | 主 | 專 | 見 |

12. major   _____

13. concentrate one's attention   _____

14. suggestion   _____

15. sit down   _____

16. important   _____

17. meet   _____

V. Dictation

18. sell four books   _____

19. You love to read Chinese books   _____

20. take a tram   _____

21. meet in the morning   _____

22. concentrate on writing   _____

23. electricity   _____

24. Mr. Wen/Man go to buy fruit   _____

Lesson 9 Column structure (1)

作信便行打次地姐門視話服

The structure of some characters may be divided into two to three columns. Do the left column first then move to the right. In each column, write from top to bottom.

Words to learn

		Radical	Meaning	Notes
1.	作 zuò jok	人	do, make	

ノ イ イ 仁 竹 竹 作 作

作							

		Radical	Meaning	Notes
2.	信 xìn seun	人	letter, trust	

ノ イ イ 仁 信 信 信 信 信

信							

3. 便 biàn   人   handy, if then
        bihn

丿 亻 仁 仃 佢 佢 佢 便 便

4. 行 xíng   行   go, travel,
        háng   O.K.
        hàhng
        hòhng

丿 彳 彳 仁 行 行

5. 打 dǎ   手   hit, beat
        dá

一 寸 才 扌 打

	Radical	*Meaning*	*Notes*

6. 次 cì / chi 欠 a classifier for occassion, time

丶 冫 汁 汐 次 次

次							

7. 地 dì / deih 土 ground

一 十 土 圵 圳 地

地							

8. 姐 jiě / jé 女 lady, sister   The horizontal stroke in the left section do not cross to the right.

乄 夊 女 奺 奵 奵 姐 姐

姐							

	Radical	Meaning	Notes

9. 門 mén 門 door
   mùhn

丨 冂 冂 冃 冃 冃 冃 門

門							

10. 視 shì 見 vision, sight,
    sih look at

丶 ㇇ 礻 礻 礻 初 初 相 相 視 視

視							

11. 話 huà 言 word, talk
    wah

丶 一 亠 亖 言 言 言 訂 訐 訐 話 話

話							

		Radical	Meaning		Notes

12. 服 fú 月 clothes, obey
　　　 fuhk

丿 刀 月 月 刖 肥 服 服

服								

Phrases to learn

		Romanization	*Meaning*
1.	工作	gōng zuò gūng jok	job, work
2.	作家	zuò jiā jok gā	writer
3.	寫信	xiě xīn sé seun	write letter
4.	信用	xìn yòng seun yuhng	credit
5.	信心	xīn xīn seun sām	confidence
6.	方便	fāng biàn fōng bihn	convenient
7.	行人	xíng rén hàhng yàhn	pedestrian
8.	打電話	dǎ diàn huà dá dihn wá	make a phone call

9.	打字	dǎ zì dá jih	typing
10.	看電視	kàn diàn shì hon dihn sih	watch television
11.	地方	dì fang deih fōng	place, space
12.	小姐	xiǎo jie síu jé	young lady; Miss
13.	姐姐	jiě jie jé jé	elder sister
14.	大門	dà mén daaih mùhn	front door or gate, main entrance
15.	門口	mén kǒu mùhn háu	doorway, entrance
16.	衣服	yī fu yī fuhk	clothes

Exercise

I. Count the number of strokes

1. 便   2. 服   3. 地   4. 門

II. Write a Chinese character with the given strokes

5. 衤 _____   6. 亻 _____   7. 千 _____

8. 西 _____   9. 日 _____   10. 田 _____

III. Choose the best meaning of the phrases

11.　　famous writer

a) 有名作家　　　　b) 老作家

c) 作家名字　　　　d) 有名工作

12.　　have confidence

a) 有心　　　　　b) 有信心

c) 有信用　　　　d) 心信

13.　四天打一次電話

a) make a phone call within four days　　b) type "four days a telephone call"

c) make a phone call every four days　　d) make four phone calls a day

14.　門口

a) doorway　　　　b) front door

c) main entrance　　d) door

IV. Dictation

15. six thousand times　　_____

16. have credit　　_____

17. pedestrian   _____

18. place   _____

19. writer   _____

20. clothes   _____

V. Fill in the blanks

21. 我今天看見你 _____ 。

I saw you <u>typing</u> today.

22. 買票很 _____ 。

It is very <u>convenient</u> to buy tickets.

23. 有空 _____ 。

Have free time to <u>watch television</u>.

24. 方先生常常寫 _____ 。

Mr. Fang/Fong often writes <u>business letter</u>.

III. Matching

25.	太方便	•	• a) writer
26.	小姐	•	• b) sister
27.	寫信	•	• c) work diligently
28.	作家	•	• d) too convenient
29.	兩次	•	• e) young lady
30.	姐姐	•	• f) write letter
31.	用心工作	•	• g) main entrance
32.	大門	•	• h) twice

Lesson 10 Column structure (2)

吃利外別期站銀飯樓點我班

Words to learn

			Radical	Meaning		Notes

1.

吃   chī   口   eat
    hek

丶 𠂆 口

吃						

2.

利   lì   刀   sharp, benefit
   leih

丿 二 千 禾 禾 利 利

利						

| | | *Radical* | *Meaning* | *Notes* |

3. 別 bié 刀   leave,
       biht   difference,
                 other, do not

丶 ㅗ 口 尸 另 別 別

別							

4. 外 wài 夕   outside,
       ngoih   foreign

丿 ㄅ 夕 列 外

外							

5. 期 qī 月   period, stage
       kèih

一 十 廾 卄 甘 甘 其 其 朞 期 期 期

期							

	Radical	Meaning	Notes

6. 站 zhàn jaahm 立 stand, station

丶 亠 丷 立 立 立 立 立 站 站 站

站						

7. 銀 yín ngàhn 金 silver

丿 𠂉 𠂉 牛 牛 余 金 金 釘 釘 釘 鈤 鈤 銀 銀

銀						

8. 飯 fàn faahn 食 rice

丿 𠂉 𠂉 牛 牛 食 食 食 飠 飠 飯 飯

飯						

	Radical	Meaning	Notes

9. 樓 lóu / làuh / láu 木 storey, building In the right column, the vertical stroke should go all the way from top to bottom.

一 十 才 才 木 杧 杧 杧 棹 椑 椐 樓 樓 樓 樓

樓							

10. 點 diǎn / dím 黑 point, dot, o'clock

丶 卜 丨 冂 曰 甲 甲 里 里 黑 黑 黑 黙 點 點 點 點

點							

11. 我 wǒ / ngóh 戈 I, me

丿 二 于 手 我 我 我

我							

		Radical	Meaning		Notes

12. 班 bān 玉 class
   bāan

一 二 千 王 玉 玨 珂 珡 班 班

班						

Phrases to learn

		Romanization	Meaning
1.	小吃	xiǎo chī síu hek	snack
2.	吃飯	chī fàn hek faahn	eat rice, eat a meal
3.	早飯	zǎo fàn jóu faahn	breakfast
4.	午飯	wǔ fàn ńgh faahn	lunch
5.	利用	lì yòng leih yuhng	use, make use of, utilize
6.	意大利	yì dà lì yi daaih leih	Italy
7.	別人	bié ren biht yàhn	other people
8.	分別	fēn bié fān biht	leave each other, difference, distinguish

9.	日期	rì qī yaht kèih	date
10.	火車站	huǒ chē zhàn fó chè jaahm	railway station
11.	銀行	yín háng ngàhn hòhng	bank
12.	樓上	lóu shàng làuh seuhng	upstairs
13.	樓下	lóu xià làuh hah	downstairs
14.	七樓	qī lóu chāt láu	seventh floor
15.	點心	diǎn xin dím sām	pastry, light refreshments
16.	一點	yī diǎn yāt dím	(colloquial) one o'clock, a little
17.	上班	shàng bān séuhng bāan	go to work
18.	下班	xià bāan hah bāan	leave work

Days of a week

1.	星期一	xīng qī yī sīng kèih yāt	Monday
2.	星期二	xīng qī èr sīng kèih yih	Tuesday
3.	星期三	xīng qī sān sīng kèih sàam	Wednesday
4.	星期四	xīng qī sì sīng kèih sei	Thursday

5.	星期五	xīng qī wǔ sīng kèih nǵh	Friday
6.	星期六	xīng qī liù sīng kèih luhk	Saturday
7.	星期日(天)	xīng qī rì (tiān) sīng kèih yaht (tīn)	Sunday

Exercise

I. Choose the correct stroke order

1.   a) ⺀ 丶 口 吒 吃 吃   b) ノ ⺀ 乞 㐅 吃 吃
     c) ㇗ 冂 口 口一 口⺊ 吃   d) ⺀ 冂 口 口ノ 口⺀ 吃

2.   a) ノ ク タ 夕丶 外   b) ノ ク 夕 列 外
     c) 丨 卜 ⺊ 外 外   d) フ ク 夕 列 外

3.   a) ⺀ 二 于 手 扟 我 我   b) ⺀ 丁 于 手 扟 我 我
     c) 一 二 于 手 扟 我 我   d) ⺀ 二 于 扟 扟 我 我

II. Fill in the missing strokes

4. 我 愛口 心 一 刂菜。

I like to <u>eat Italian</u> food.

5. ⺀ 丿 ⼂ 彡 的 電 話。

<u>Make use of</u> the telephone at the <u>bank</u>.

6. 女 ⼀ 有 書 賣 。

There are books for sale <u>downstairs</u>.

7. 曰 月 ⼆ 要 ⼀ 王 。

We need to <u>go to work</u> on <u>Wednesday</u>.

8. 今 天 丶 口 ＇ ⼁ ⼀ 外 見 。

Meet you outside the <u>train station</u> at <u>six o'clock</u> today.

III. Write the following time expressions

9. 17th June Monday _____

10. 21st December Sunday _____

11. 30th May, 1989 _____

12. 15th April, 1976 _____

13. 28th March Thursday _____

IV. Choose the best meaning of the phrases

14.   go to work by car

    a) 坐車去出班   b) 坐車去上班

    c) 上車去下班   d) 下車去上班

15. 7:25 a.m.

    a) 上午七點二十五分   b) 下午七點二十五分
    c) 中午七點兩十五分   d) 正午七點兩十五分

16. delicious snacks

    a) 可口大吃   b) 美口中吃
    c) 可口小吃   d) 美口吃

17. I have lunch at 1:00.

    a) 我午飯吃一點   b) 我一點午飯吃
    c) 我吃午飯一點   d) 我一點吃午飯

18. next Sunday

    a) 下一星期   b) 下星期七
    c) 下星期日   d) 下天星期

V. Dictation

19. eat something   _____

20. I love you   _____

21. last Thursday   _____

22. 18th floor   _____

84

23. buy (some) pastry home   _____

24. breakfast   _____

VI. Write a Chinese character with the given strokes

25. 口 _____   26. 月 _____

27. 刂 _____   28. 王 _____

Lesson 11 Complicated structures

特時晚情路後滿新街前學國

To write more complicated charactérs, divide the character either into columns or layers. Divide each column into top , middle and bottom sections. Then write layer by layer. Divide each layer into left, middle and right sections, then write column by column.

Words to learn

		Radical	Meaning	Notes
1.	特 tè dahk	牛	special	

特

時							

		Radical	Meaning	Notes
2.	時 shí sih	日	time, o'clock	

時

時							

3. 晚 wǎn   日   night, evening
        máahn

丨 冂 冂 日 日′ 旷 旷 旷 旷 晚 晚

晚						

4. 情 qíng   心   feeling
        chìhng

丶 丨 忄 忄 忙 忙 忭 恃 情 情 情

情						

5. 路 lù   足   road
        louh

丶 丨 口 口 早 早 昆 足 足′ 跗 跕 路 路

路						

	Radical	Meaning	Notes

6. 後 hòu / hauh 彳 back, behind

丿 ㇇ 彳 彳' 갸 갸 갸 後 後

後							

7. 滿 mǎn / múhn 水 full, fill up

丶 丶 氵 汀 汀 汀 汫 滿 滿 滿 滿 滿

滿							

8. 新 xīn / sān 斤 new

丶 亠 六 古 立 立 辛 辛 亲 亲 新 新 新

新							

	Radical	Meaning		Notes

9. 街 jīe gāai　　行　　street

ノ ｲ ｲ ｲ 彳 衧 徏 徏 徍 徍 街 街

街						

10. 前 qián chìhn　　刀　　front, before　　Firstly write the top layer, then write the bottom left and right columns.

丶 丷 亠 广 广 丷 前 前 前

前						

11. 學 xué hohk　　子　　learn, school　　Divide the top into three bars. Write from left to right.

ˊ ｆ ｆ ｆ ｆ 臼 臼 臼 臼 臼 臼 臼 臼 學 學 學

學						

		Radical	Meaning		Notes

12. 國　guó　口　country
　　　　gwok

丨 冂 冂 冂 冃 冋 冏 國 國 國 國

國						

Phrases to learn

		Romanization	Meaning
1.	特別	tè bié dahk biht	special
2.	一時十分	yī shí shí fēn yāt sìh sahp fān	(time) 1:05
3.	兩小時	liǎng xiǎo shí léuhng síu sìh	two hours
4.	晚上	wán shàng máahn seuhng	in the evening, at night
5.	晚飯	wán fàn máahn faahn	dinner
6.	心情	xīn qíng sām chìhng	mood, state of mind
7.	事情	shì qíng sih chìhng	matter, affair
8.	走路	zǒu lù jáu louh	walk

9.	後面	hòu miàn hauh mihn	at the back, behind
10.	以後	yǐ hòu yíh hauh	after, afterwards
11.	滿意	mǎn yì múhn yi	satisfy, contented
12.	新年	xīn nián sān nìhn	New Year
13.	上街	shàng jiē séuhng gāai	go into the street, go shopping
14.	前天	qián tiān chìhn tīn	day before yesterday
15.	上學	shàng xué séuhng hohk	go to school
16.	學生	xué shēng hohk sàng	student
17.	大學	dà xué daaih hohk	university
18.	國家	guó jiā gwok gā	country
19.	中國	zhōng guó jùng gwok	China
20.	美國	měi guó méih gwok	America

Exercise

I. Count the number of strokes of the following characters

1. 前   2. 晚   3. 後   4. 街

II. Choose the best meaning of the phrases

5.　　上小學
  　　a) there is a little school above　　b) learn a little from school
  　　c) go to primary school　　d) a few students go up

6.　　8:40 am.
  　　a) 上午八時四分　　b) 下午八時十四分
  　　c) 上午八時四十分　　d) 上午八時十四分

7.　　My sister writes letter tonight
  　　a) 今早我姐姐寫書　　b) 今天我姐姐寫信
  　　c) 今晚我姐姐寫信　　d) 今年我姐姐去日本

8.　　work for more than ten hours
  　　a) 工作十小時以上　　b) 十小時以下工作
  　　c) 十一時工作　　d) 一天工作十小時

III. Write the following time expressions

9. 12:00 noon　　_____

10. just 3:00 p.m.　　_____

11. 6:30 a.m.　　_____

12. 5:29 p.m.　　_____

13. 11:48 at night   _____

14. 7 hours   _____

15. 2.5 hours   _____

IV. Fill in the blanks

16. _____ 愛吃牛肉。

    <u>Americans</u> like to eat beef.

17. 我天天上 _____ 。

    I go to <u>university</u> every day.

18. 車小姐 _____ 買新衣。

    Miss Che buy new clothes for <u>New Year</u>.

V. Matching

19. 滿分 •	•	a) full marks
20. 中國 •	•	b) October of the year before last
21. 小學生 •	•	c) important matter
22. 大街 •	•	d) China
23. 前年十月 •	•	e) main street
24. 重要事情 •	•	f) primary school student

VI. Dictation

25. go into the street   _____

26. walk home   _____

27. after this year   _____

28. mood   _____

29. satisfy   _____

30. special meaning   _____

Lesson 12 "Clam shell" structure

店原病房間開氣起道進運過

The structure of some characters is like a clam shell, with the outer enclosing the inner section. Write the outer section first, then write the inner section.

Words to learn

		Radical	*Meaning*	*Notes*
1.	店 diàn dim	广	shop	

丶 亠 广 广 广 庐 庐 店 店

店						

2.	原 yuán yùhn	厂	original, former	

一 厂 厂 厂 厂 厅 庐 盾 原 原 原

原						

| | Radical | Meaning | Notes |

3. 病 bìng
behng;
bihng   疒   sick, illness

丶 亠 广 广 疒 疒 疒 病 病 病

病								

4. 房 fáng
fòhng   戶   house, room

丶 亠 ゔ 户 户 户 房 房

房								

5. 間 jiān
gāan   門   a classifier
for houses
and rooms,
between, among

丨 冂 冂 冃 門 門 門 門 門 間 間 間

間								

		Radical	Meaning		Notes

6. 開 kāi 門　　open
　　 hòi

｜ ｒ ｐ ｐ ｐˋ ｐˋ ｐˋ 門 門 門 閈 開

開							

7. 氣 qì　　气　　air, gas
　　 hei

ノ ＾ ＾ 气 气 气 氘 氛 氛 氣

氣							

8. 起 qǐ　　走　　get up, start　Lengthen the bottom right-falling stroke to
　　 héi　　　　　　　　　　　　 serve as a boat for the top section.

一 十 土 キ キ キ 走 走 起 起 起

起							

| | Radical | Meaning | Notes |

9. 道 dào
     douh   辵   road   Start with the top section before writing the boat-like section.

丶 丷 丷 丷 产 芍 肖 肖 首 `首 渞 道

道							

10. 進 jìn
       jeun   辵   enter, advance

丿 亻 亻 亻 亻 亻 隹 隹 `隹 谁 進

進							

11. 運 yùn
       wahn   辵   transport, luck

丶 冖 冖 冖 宀 宀 冒 宣 軍 軍 渾 運

運							

		Radical	Meaning	Notes
12.	過 guò gwo	辵	cross, pass, have experience of	

丶 冂 冂 冋 冎 咼 咼 咼 咼 過 過 過

過							

Phrases to Learn

		Romanization	Meaning
1.	商店	shāng diàn sēung dim	shop
2.	書店	shū diàn syù dim	book shop
3.	原本	yuán běn yùhn bún	originally, formerly
4.	生病	shēng bìng sàng behng	sick, ill
5.	房間	fáng jiān fòhng gāan	room
6.	中間	zhōng jiān jūng gāan	in the middle, in between
7.	時間	shí jiān sìh gaan	time
8.	走開	zǒu kāi jáu hòi	walk away

9.	開門	kāi mén hòi mùhn	open door
10.	開心	kāi xīn hōi sām	feel happy; rejoice
11.	開學	kāi xué hōi hohk	school opens, term begins
12.	天氣	tiān qì tīn hei	weather
13.	生氣	shēng qì sàng hei	angry
14.	空氣	kōng qì hūng hei	air
15.	走運	zǒu yùn jáu wahn	have good luck
16.	站起來	zhàn qi lai jaahm héi lòih	stand up
17.	道路	dào lù douh louh	road
18.	過去	guò qù gwo heui	in the past, pass by
19.	進口	jìn kǒu jeun háu	import

Exercise

I. Count the number of strokes and find out the first stroke

1. 房   2. 過   3. 病

4. 起   5. 間   6. 氣

II. Fill in the missing strokes

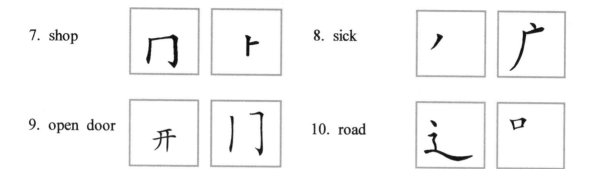

7. shop 　门　卜

8. sick 　丿　广

9. open door 　开　门

10. road 　辶　口

III. Choose the best meaning of the phrases

11. 我走進房間

    a) I run into the room   b) I am running out of time

    c) I walk into the room   d) I walk out of the room

12. 九月二十四日起

    a) start from 24th September

    b) stand up for nine months and twenty four days

    c) get up on 24th September

    d) last for nine months and twenty four days

13. 過重

    a) I was once heavy   b) overweight

    c) pass time   d) miss something important

14. 第九間分店

    a) No. 9 book shop   b) consignment No. 9

    c) split into nine shops   d) the 9th branch store

15. 空運

   a) no luck

   b) something is moving in the sky

   c) deliver by air

   d) nothing has been send

16. back door

   a) 開門

   b) 大門

   c) 前門

   d) 後門

IV. Fill in the blanks

17. 我 _____ 去打電話。

   I <u>stand up</u> and go to make a phone call.

18. 一百五十間 _____ 。

   150 <u>book stores</u>

19. 八月十五日 _____ 。

   The <u>school term starts</u> from 15th of August.

V. Dictation

20. originally _____

21. have good luck _____

22. in the middle　　　　　_____

23. angry　　　　　　　　_____

24. imported beef　　　　　_____

25. in the past　　　　　　_____

26. walk away　　　　　　_____

27. 4000 rooms　　　　　　_____

28. weather　　　　　　　_____

29. happy　　　　　　　　_____

30. dinner time　　　　　　_____

Answers

Lesson 1

1. c	2. a	3. c	4. b	5. b	6. b
7. d	8. a	9. d	10. b	11. e	12. f
13. g	14. c	15. a	16. 牛	17. 二十二	

18. 三千年　　19. 生　　20. 正

Lesson 2

1. d	2. b	3. d	4. b	5. b	6. a
7. c	8. d	9. c	10. a	11. f	12. g
13. d	14. a	15. c	16. b	17. e	18. h

19. 火　　20. 人生　　21. 太大　　22. 十天半

23. 入　　24. 主人

Lesson 3

1. a	2. b	3. c	4. a	5. c	6. b
7. d	8. b	9. d	10. d	11. h	12. d
13. a	14. f	15. g	16. b	17. e	18. c

19. 友人　　20. 二千八百五十七天　　21. 入口

22. 中文　　23. 出生　　24. 出去

Lesson 4

1. a	2. d	3. d	4. c	5. b	6. a
7. c	8. c	9. a	10. d	11. b	12. a
13. b	14. f	15. c	16. g	17. a	18. e
19. h	20. d	21. 上月四日		22. 八十五元	

23. 可口   24. 大衣   25. 大小

Lesson 5

1. a	2. b	3. d	4. c	5. a	6. 8
7. 8	8. 8	9. 8	10. 6	11. c	12. d
13. d	14. a	15. b	16. c	17. d	18. e
19. a	20. f	21. b	22. 牛肉		23. 兩年半

24. 日本人   25. 下雨   26. 火車

Lesson 6

1. b	2. d	3. b	4. a	5. c	6. d
7. b	8. a	9. 15	10. 9	11. 9	12. 11
13. g	14. f	15. c	16. d	17. a	18. e
19. b	20. h	21. 常常		22. 天空、星星	

23. 回家   24. 你有空   25. 回來   26. 東面

27. 文字   28. 四方   29. 寫名字   30. 家人

Lesson 7

1. b	2. a	3. d	4. 13	5. 11	6. 9
7. 13	8. c	9. a	10. b	11. c	12. a

13. 工業中心　　14. 走　　15. 商業　　16. 一百分

17. 老人　　18. 男人　　19. d　　20. a　　21. b

22. c　　23. e　　24. f　　25. 有意思　　26. 十分

27. 第四年

Lesson 8

1. 13	2. 10	3. 13	4. 11	5. b	6. c
7. b	8. c	9. d	10. b	11. a	12. 主要

13. 專心　　14. 主意　　15. 坐下　　16. 重要

17. 見面　　18. 賣四本書　　19. 你愛看中文書

20. 坐電車　　21. 早上見　　22. 專心寫字

23. 電　　24. 文先生去買水果

Lesson 9

1. 9	2. 8	3. 6	4. 8	11. a	12. b
13. c	14. a	15. 六千次		16. 有信用	

17. 行人　　18. 地方　　19. 作家　　20. 衣服

21. 打字　　22. 方便　　23. 看電視　　24. 商業信

25. d　　26. e　　27. f　　28. a　　29. h　　30. b

31. c　　32. g

Lesson 10

1. d　　2. b　　3. a　　4. 吃意大利

5. 利用、銀行　　6. 樓下　　7. 星期三、上班

8. 六點、火車站

9. 六月十七日　星期一

10. 十二月二十一日　星期日

11. 一九八九年五月三十日

12. 一九七六年四月十五日

13. 三月二十八日　星期四

14. b　　15. a　　16. c　　17. d　　18. c

19. 吃東西　　20. 我愛你　　21. 上星期四

22. 十八樓　　23. 買點心回家　　24. 早飯

Lesson 11

1. 9　　2. 11　　3. 9　　4. 12　　5. c　　6. c

7. c　　8. a　　9. 中午十二時　　10. 三時正

11. 上午六時半　　　12. 下午五時二十九分

13. 晚上十一時四十八分　　　14. 七小時

15. 兩小時半　　　16. 美國人　　　17. 大學

18. 新年　　　19. a　　　20. d　　　21. f　　　22. e　　　23. b

24. c　　　25. 上街　　　26. 走路回家　　　27. 今年以後

28. 心情　　　29. 滿意　　　30. 特別意思

Lesson 12

1. 8 、　　2. 13 丨　　3. 10 、　　4. 10 一　　5. 12 丨　　6. 10 丿

7. 商店　　8. 生病　　9. 開門　　10. 道路　　11. c　　　12. a

13. b　　　14. d　　　15. c　　　16. d　　　17. 站起來

18. 書店　　　19. 開學　　　20. 原本

21. 走運　　　22. 中間　　　23. 生氣　　　24. 進口牛肉

25. 過去　　　26. 走開　　　27. 四千間房間

28. 天氣　　　29. 開心　　　30. 晚飯時間

Appendix I Table of simplified characters

In this book, we have learned how to write traditional Chinese characters. In Mainland China and Singapore, a simplified form of Chinese characters is being used. Traditional characters and simplified characters share many characteristics. The following chart gives a list of those characters learned in this book that have simplified forms. In each column the characters on the left side is the traditional form and it's simplified form is shown on the right.

T ⇋ S	T ⇋ S	T ⇋ S
來 ⇋ 来	愛 ⇋ 爱	滿 ⇋ 满
兩 ⇋ 两	門 ⇋ 门	學 ⇋ 学
寫 ⇋ 写	視 ⇋ 视	國 ⇋ 国
業 ⇋ 业	話 ⇋ 话	間 ⇋ 间
書 ⇋ 书	銀 ⇋ 银	開 ⇋ 开
見 ⇋ 见	飯 ⇋ 饭	氣 ⇋ 气
買 ⇋ 买	樓 ⇋ 楼	進 ⇋ 进
賣 ⇋ 卖	點 ⇋ 点	運 ⇋ 运
專 ⇋ 专	後 ⇋ 后	過 ⇋ 过
電 ⇋ 电		

Appendix II More characters to learn

仁	汁	計	支	枝	技	古	沽	姑
rén yàhn *kernel, humanity*	zhī jāp *juice*	jì gai *calculate, plan*	zhī jī *support*	zhī jī *branch*	jì geih *technique, skill*	gǔ gú *ancient*	gū gū *sell*	gū gū *aunt*

枯	苦	固	個	故	做	湖	朝	潮
kū fū *withered*	kǔ fú *bitter*	gù gu *firm*	gè go *classifier for objects & people*	gù gu *reason, cause*	zuò jouh *do*	hú wùh *lake*	zhāo; cháo jiu; chìuh *morning; face*	cháo chìuh *tide*

乾	合	哈	洽	拾	答	茶	刀	份
gān gōn *dry*	hé hahp *joint, shut*	hā hā *roar with laughter*	qià hāp *be in harmony, consult*	shí sahp *pick up*	dá; dā daap *answer*	chá chah *tea*	dāo dōu *knife*	fèn fahn *components*

招	照	超	力	加	另	功	助	架
zhāo jīu *enrol, beckon*	zhào jiu *photograph, according to*	chāo chīu *exceed*	lì lihk *power*	jiā gā *add*	lìng lihng *other*	gōng gūng *skill, result*	zhù joh *help*	jià ga *shelf, frame*

丁	訂	何	河	奇	寄	椅	哥	歌
dīng dīng *man, fourth*	dìng dihng *subscribe, reserve*	hé hòh *what, why, a surname*	hé hòh *river*	qí kèih *strange*	jì gei *mail*	yǐ yí *chair*	gē gō *elder brother*	gē gō *song*

又	受	反	板	左	右	若	灰	恢
yòu	shòu	fǎn	bǎn	zuǒ	yòu	ruò	huī	huī
yauh	sauh	faan	baan	jó	yauh	yeuhk	fūi	fūi
again	*receive*	*opposite*	*board*	*left*	*right*	*if, as*	*grey, ash*	*extensive*

丸	充	育	江	士	吉	周	週	調
wán	chōng	yù	jiāng	shì	jí	zhōu	zhōu	tiáo; diào
yún	chūng	yuhk	gōng	sih	gāt	jāu	jāu	tiùh; diuh
pill, ball	*fill, sufficient*	*raise*	*river*	*scholar*	*good fortune*	*all over*	*week, cycle*	*adjust; tone*

犬	因	尖	京	涼	諒	景	影	叔
quǎn	yīn	jiān	jīng	liáng	liàng	jǐng	yǐng	shū
hyun	yān	jīm	gīng	lèuhng	leuhng	gíng	yíng	sūk
dog	*because*	*point*	*capital*	*cool*	*forgive*	*scenery*	*shadow*	*uncle*

少	沙	抄	妙	吵	秒	鈔	省	乞
shǎo; shào	shā	chāo	miào	chǎo; chāu	miǎo	chāo	shěng; xǐng	qǐ
síu; siu	sā	chāau	miuh	cháau	míuh	chāau	sáang; síng	hāt
few; young	*sand*	*transscriibe, take down*	*wonderful, clever*	*make a noise*	*second*	*bank note*	*province, save; introspect*	*beg*

巾	布	佈	吊	也	他	她	池	牠
jīn	bù	bù	diào	yě	tā	tā	chí	tā
gān	bou	bou	diu	yáh	tā	tā	chìh	tā
towel	*cloth*	*announce*	*hang*	*also*	*he, other*	*she*	*pool*	*it*

拖	施	土	吐	肚	社	佳	掛	了
tuō	shī	tǔ	tù	dù	shè	jiā	guà	le; liǎo
tō	sī	tóu	tou	tóuh	séh	gāai	gwa	líuh
pull; drag	*grant, impose*	*earth*	*vomit*	*stomach*	*society*	*best*	*hang*	*complete*

111

子 zi jí son	李 lǐ léih plum, a surname	季 jì gwai season	孝 xiào haau filial piety	教 jiào; jiāo gaau teach	厚 hòu háuh thick	好 hǎo; hào hóu; hou good; fond of	安 ān ōn safe	如 rú yùh if, as
恕 shù syu forgive	寸 cùn chyun inch	守 shǒu sáu guard, defend	付 fù fuh pay	府 fǔ fú government office	符 fú fùh symbol	村 cūn chyūn village	封 fēng fūng seal	等 děng dáng wait etc.
待 dài; dāi doih wait; treat	持 chí chìh hold, support	傳 chuán; zhuàn chyùhn transmit; biography	團 tuán tyùhn group	轉 zhuǎn; zhuàn jyun turn	多 duō dò many	移 yí yìh move	只 zhǐ jí only	品 pǐn bán product
兄 xiōng hīng brother	祝 zhù jūk wish	克 kè hāk can, gram	扣 kòu kau button up	台 tái tòih stage	治 zhì jih cure, govern	始 shǐ chí start	怡 yí yìh cheerful, happy	抬 tái tòih lift, raise
胎 tāi tōi foetus	苔 tái tòih mosses	怠 dài tóih idle	舌 shé sit tongue	活 huó wuht live	闊 kuò fut wide	問 wèn mahn ask	佔 zhàn jim occupy	帖 tiě tip invitation
貼 tiē tip paste	捐 juān gyūn donate	同 tóng tùhng together	洞 dòng duhng hole	詞 cí chìh phrase	杏 xing hahng almond	呆 dāi ngòih dull	保 bǎo bóu protect, guarantee	堡 bǎo bóu fortress

告	造	哭	單	禪	各	格	客	落
gào gou *tell, accuse*	zào jouh *make, create*	kū hūk *cry*	dān dāan *single*	chán sìhm *zen*	gè gok *each*	gé gaak *division check*	kè haak *guest, customer*	luò lohk *fall, lower*
閣	戶	肩	淚	王	旺	住	往	注
gé gok *pavilion*	hù wuh *account*	jiān gīn *shoulder*	lèi leuih *tears*	wáng wòhng *king*	wàng wohng *prosperous*	zhù jyuh *live, stay*	wàng; wǎng wóhng *go to*	zhù jyu *concentrate on, pour*
冲	忠	串	志	急	想	怎	昨	明
chōng chūng *pour boiling water*	zhōng jūng *loyal*	chuàn chyun *string together*	zhì ji *will, ideal*	jí gāp *urgent*	xiǎng séung *think, wish*	zěn jám *how*	zuó johk *yesterday*	míng mìhng *bright*
晶	指	草	但	查	宣	昌	唱	朋
jīng jīng *crystal*	zhǐ jí *finger, point at*	cǎo chóu *grass*	dàn daahn *but*	chá chàh *investigate*	xuān syūn *announce*	chāng chēung *prosperous*	chàng cheung *sing*	péng pàhng *friend*
止	企	扯	址	肯	政	症	完	玩
zhǐ jí *stop*	qǐ kéih *look forward to*	chě ché *pull*	zhǐ jí *address*	kěn háng *willing to*	zhèng jing *politics*	zhèng jing *illness*	wán yùhn *finish*	wán wuhn *play*
欠	吹	欣	斤	折	近	放	敗	數
qiàn him *owe*	chuī chēui *blow*	xīn yān *joyful*	jīn gān *606 g*	zhé jit *break, discount*	jìn gahn *near, close*	fàng fong *put down*	bài baaih *lose*	shù ;shǔ sou; sóu *number; count*

件	含	念	琴	令	冷	零	木	林
jiàn	hán	niàn	qín	lìng	lěng	líng	mù	lín
gihn	hàhm	nihm	kàhm	lihng	láahng	lìhng	muhk	làhm
piece	contain	study, read, miss	a musical instrument	order	cold	zero	wood	forest

麻	禁	森	桌	梨	樂	困	相	箱
má	jìn	sēn	zhuō	lí	lè ;yuè	kùn	xiāng	xiāng
màh	gam	sām	cheuk	lèih	lohk; ngohk	kwan	sēung	sēung
linen	forbid	jungle	table	pear	happy; music	difficulty	each other	box

表	青	清	晴	睛	請	足	促	捉
biǎo	qīng	qīng	qíng	jīng	qǐng	zú	cù	zhuō
bíu	chīng	chīng	chìhng	jīng	chíng	jūk	chūk	jūk
surface, express, table	blue, green	clear	fine weather	eye	please, invite	foot, enough	urge	catch

定	是	提	伴	胖	丙	白	皇	泉
dìng	shì	dī; tí	bàn	pàng	bǐng	bái	huáng	quán
dihng	sih	tàih	buhn	buhn	bíng	baahk	wòhng	chyùhn
decide, stable	yes	mention	accompany	fat	third	white, in vain	imperial, emperor	water spring

棉	伯	怕	拍	目	着	自	息	臭
mián	bó	pà	pāi	mù	zhe; zháo	zì	xī	chòu
mìhn	baak	pa	paak	muhk	jeuhk	jih	sīk	chau
cotton	uncle	afraid	clap, pat	eye, item	~ing, touch	oneself	breath, interest	smelly

宜	租	祖	性	姓	示	宗	弟	梯
yí	zū	zǔ	xìng	xìng	shì	zōng	dì	tī
yìh	jōu	jóu	sing	sing	sih	jūng	daih	tāi
suitable;	rent	ancestor	sex, type	surname	show	ancestor; faction	younger brother	ladder; staircase

禾	私	和	香	秋	法	立	辛	位
hé wòh *crops*	sī sī *private*	hé wòh *and*	xiāng hēung *fragrant*	qiū chāu *autumn*	fǎ faat *method*	lì lahp *stand*	xīn sān *hot, suffering*	wèi wái; waih *position*
倍	音	暗	接	章	境	鏡	億	憶
bèi púih *times*	yīn yām *sound*	àn am *dark*	jiē jip *receive*	zhāng jēung *stamp, chapter*	jìng gíng *territory*	jìng geng *mirror*	yì yīk *100000000*	yì yīk *recall*
田	副	富	福	逼	當	米	迷	畫
tián tìhn *field*	fù fu *deputy, subsidary*	fù fu *rich*	fú fūk *good fortune*	bī bīk *force*	dāng dōng *work as*	mǐ máih *rice*	mí màih *lost*	huà waahk ;wá *draw; picture*
良	浪	很	恨	娘	根	眼	跟	踏
liáng lèuhng *well*	làng lohng *wave*	hěn hán *quite*	hèn hahn *hate*	niáng nèuhng *mother*	gēn gān *root*	yǎn ngáahn *eye*	gēn gān *follow*	tà ; tā daahp *step on*
洗	更	赴	餓	現	親	覺	貝	貴
xǐ sái *wash*	gèng; gēng gang; gàng *more; replace*	fù fuh *go to*	è ngoh *hungry*	xiàn yihn *now*	qīn chān *parent, relative*	jué; jiào gok; gaau *feel; sleep*	bèi bui *shell*	guì gwai *expensive*
負	責	價	員	圓	損	賞	裳	嘗
fù fuh *bear*	zé jaak *duty*	jià ga *price*	yuán yùhn *member*	yuán yùhn *round*	sún syún *lose, damage*	shǎng séung *reward, appreciate*	cháng sèuhng *clothes*	cháng sèuhng *tasete, try*

座	彩	採	其	棋	旗	准	隻	雙
zuò	cǎi	cǎi	qí	qí	qí	zhǔn	zhī	shuāng
joh	chói	chói	kèih	kèih	kèih	jén	jek	sēung
block	colourful	pick	his, her, that	chess	flag	allow	classifier for animals	pair
堆	推	售	集	準	誰	這	語	課
duī	tuī	shòu	jí	zhǔn	shúi	zhè	yǔ	kè
dēui	tēui	sauh	jaahp	jéun	sèuih	jé	yúh	fo
heap, pile	push	sell	gather	accurate, prepare	who	this	language	lesson, course
兔	軟	連	輛	倆	雪	雷	霜	露
tù	ruǎn	lián	liàng	liǎ	xuě	léi	shuāng	lù
tou	yúhn	lìhn	leuhng	léuhng	syut	lèuih	sēung	louh
rabbit	soft	link	classifier for cars	two of us	snow	thunder	frost	dew, reveal
金	閃	們	悶	間	簡	或	動	種
jīn	shǎn	men	mèn	jiān	jiǎn	huò	dòng	zhǒng; zhòng
gām	sím	mùhn	muhn	gāan	gáan	waahk	duhng	júng; jung
gold	flash	indicate people in plural	boring	among, between room	simple	or	move	type; plant
董	懂	禍	鍋	剪	煎	黑	墨	默
dǒng	dǒng	huò	guō	jiǎn	jiān	hēi	mò	mò
dúng	dúng	woh	wō	jín	jīn	hāk	mahk	mahk
a surname	understand	disaster	pot	cut	pan fry	black	ink	silent

Flash cards: Components of Chinese characters

一	二	丨	卜	八	儿
冫	丿	夂	㞢	四	圭
西	虫	乂	匕	厶	儿
夂	月	灬	长	乄	幺
开	电	豖	亻	彳	冖
氵	才	忄	礻	牜	足
另	食	刂	卜	宁	夂
艮	乍	尔	艮	佳	咼

四 空	六	主		元 二 三	天 百 一 三
情	買 賣	先 元			千
先	去 公	老	文	專	要 票
後	走	衣		有 前 情	愛 路 後
次	行 後 街	作 便 信 你 視	家	電	開
路	特		情	打	滿
	行 街	外	利 前 別 你	飯	別
過	進	銀	你	作	服

Flash cards: Components of Chinese characters

妻	㒼	刀	力	又	九
人	入	七	八	十	十
大	工	士	千	子	小
也	巾	寸	乞	上	下
女	土	土	夕	夕	口
吅	方	欠	止	反	中
斤	今	五	水	午	牛
火	心	王	王	木	林

九	友	男	分	滿	樓
十 早		八 分	七	入	人
小 原 下	字 學 上	千 話 吃	賣	工 空 市 常	大 天 太 地
口 話 名 名 中	名 飯	正	專 特 時 街 特 時 次	街 方 房	女 姐
牛	午	水	五	今	新
	樓 新	主		心 思 意 愛	火

120

Flash cards: Components of Chinese characters

月	月	日	晶	曰	昌
目	白	禾	且	占	立
丙	示	田	生	用	司
半	出	以	本	弟	米
年	西	肉	采	更	免
言	車	貝	見	我	坐
或	其	金	來	兩	雨
首	重	東	果	事	軍

	早 星 書 意		晚 間 時	月 服 期	
新 意 站	點 店	姐	利	百 原	
司	用	生 星	男 思	票	病
氣	第	本	以	出	半
晚	便	菜	肉	西	年
坐	我	見 視	買 賣	車	信 話
雨	兩	來	銀	期	國
運	事	果	東	重	道

Flash cards: Components of Chinese characters

面 看 班 起 宀 聿

商 黑 寫 業 羊 尚

人 二 ナ

丁 厂 广

门 几 口

書	家 字 空	起	班	看	面
常	美	業	寫	點	商

友		六 文	市 衣	人	
店		原		可	
回 四 國					

Flash cards: Components of Chinese characters

房	氣	前
道 進 運 過	愛	老
病	第	菜
學	門 間 開	電